D0224575

SIDEBROW BOOKS

VALLEY FEVER

Published by Sidebrow Books
P.O. Box 86921
Portland, OR 97286
sidebrow@sidebrow.net
www.sidebrow.net

Cover art by Alex Roulette ("Crossroads")
Cover & book design by Jason Snyder

ISBN: 1-940090-03-2
ISBN-13: 978-1-940090-03-0

FIRST EDITION | FIRST PRINTING
9 8 7 6 5 4 3 2 1
SIDEBROW BOOKS 014
PRINTED IN THE UNITED STATES

Sidebrow Books titles are distributed by
Small Press Distribution

Titles are available directly from Sidebrow at
www.sidebrow.net/books

A Member of

Sidebrow is a member of the Intersection Incubator, a program of
Intersection for the Arts (www.theintersection.org) providing fiscal
sponsorship, incubation, and consulting for artists. Contributions
to Sidebrow are tax-deductible to the extent allowed by law.

VALLEY FEVER

JULIA BLOCH

SIDEBROW BOOKS + 2015 + PORTLAND & SAN FRANCISCO

I'm sick to death of this particular self.
I want another.

—Virginia Woolf, *Orlando*

THE SELFIST

WELCOME ABROAD

I had a feeling of wanting to walk
the way I was told to walk.

But everyone worries and rents
and swivels as little machines.

After the first haircut the left side kind
of looks OK but the right side looks like shit.

I had a feeling of wanting to protect my joint.
A seabird moved north on one leg, another

aimed at his tail feathers, it is hard
to forget these things unless it isn't.

Bonnard's nude happened in the past, she is
on the bed with red threads,

she was once owned by Stein, and this
museum's filled with a future feeling.

OCCLUSIONARY

Compositionally, one could take this angle
of the apartment and turn it to the greeny

decay beyond the window, squirrel
shouting on branch, paint lathered

much younger than what it borders,
silver spacing out the wall.

Person at metal desk thinks Leonid showers
must create a bright sort of clutter, that

person tracks the motion of lead, an
impatient eye submerges order under

glass, arrows splinter the lead
trucking in need through the fall.

Dust of the heart and spine.
Lead filtering a city.

SCORDATURA

Tipped futurity, ash
as snowflake, a dress one gets
laid in, a species of plastic
that shines before an off-
tuned face, I mean your
slackish mouth and the slightly
separate set of strings it cuts
itself on, tuned just a few
degrees northwest toward this
upper right hand, inherently
clean. "They have a sea there"
the cabbie said on the way
to the affective subway as I
stroked your temporal bone.

SKYTIME

Shopping lights string the street
under a graying sky

I'm not sure you understand
love as viewed from a strange city

Noisome maidenhair littering the sidewalk
a personality lacking chirpiness

Whereas others mouth red words
linen drapes around this window

The tongue, a lieful
upon this cellphone

I don't want the sweater anymore, it
constricts the thorax

I'll be an ingratefull seasoner
sewing it onto the dark

APARTMENT

Of bother. Smooth bowls in winter,
winter on edge of something altering fast.
At 18th Street, black pen
hemmed into notebook, lady on bus
says "Knock it off, the subway is down."
A clench that mimics the city, a building's
opposite account of glare.

We choose the hit for envy's sake. Seabirds
are serene unless they're flying. Stiff fingers
in cold fog, a mouth working itself
before a camera. The replacement, however.
The lady says "I have a king, I have a king."
An animal moves inside the old wall that
divides something living from something
dying, no matter how many times
we wash it.

LEVEL

A view from the train, as if a mixture
of trees organized the water, or
a face over the surface of

a new set of structures in the water.
One object hinges into another
and we know it like ethicality,

if only from a long view. There may
be this view from a train,
or the cooling effects of a train in winter

inflecting sight, an altered tree,
distance filtered from
new structures, fibrous or laminate.

I did hear on the radio about a "bad little
cloud," I did "click here to like this." Then
I watched the spilling trees.

DEAR MARY McDONNELL

You've ornamented your hair
with red shelves. The effect
looks cluttered, but
astronomical, the way
a ship with no sails finds
traction on waves like
question marks. I am rather
cold up here, I am parted
by the hurrying world.
Leave the commentary
to busy laborers. Your
battlestar betrays
a melancholy slackening
beneath its skirt.

THE BYRONIC WOMAN

I love a woman whose
face is about to cry

I don't love it if she cries
only if she is about to

I've really only noticed this in the movies
like Mimi Rogers in *Lost in Space*

Like when a woman speaks
and it catches in your throat

Mimi Rogers holds the stylus,
protests the departure

I watch the globes at her throat
orbit along a smooth blue line

She is on the bed
of wires

Her hair rises over her collar
like a sea

I am sore sick at heart, I have
almost long'd for woe

THE TIGHT PANTS OF THE ARTS

Fashioning that red cloud
into the other museum.

I am too old to remember that song.
I mean in the way you do so fondly.

I'm on the blind cellphone
loosening the circuitry.

Here's a carbonized new decade
and its ectopic embrace.

Decades go on. We'll catch up
eventually. Meanwhile let's overcook
the food, let's clutter up our salads

and your upright face.

OCCASIONARY

Last night's storm throws
up small drops against
the big clay-colored building
that houses those oily
paintings, those Dutch
copies releasing energy
into the wan afternoon.
The day seems plaqued. We
don't want to stink of need. I
thought the statue on the path
was a hanged person. A huge
middle is not the same as
a center, unfortunately.

PST SONNET

A glass hug. A shaken sense. Even your shirt
was lying. Your whole body full of liquid. I there
is a word blocking the bow. I there is to go
shortly. A there bar. A there sacroiliac joint. Let's to
the stone gallery. A video, *Ball Drop*, 1969, a ball
turns upon a windshield and smash. Like that.
So let's ransom this hotel, let's put a fee upon this
feeling. Nah. Too various century. Look up all the
bones of the body to see what you can spare.
Dark, grey-green. Not everything can be cited.
I must needs.
Green face lies.
Fall apart for the day.
Like I said, a glass hug.

NATIONAL GALLERY

Grassy paint at the edge sinking
like a claw. Eve of Christmas
Eve, and wet. Just sit there and
watch art, and read Jameson,
and celebrate Christ. There's a dead
wreath in the mirror, right next
to a face. Let's talk about
the spotlit Hoppers, sure. Or
the seaside paint across
the street. It's past the gift shop.
"You have a very fiery temper
according to your hands."

TONAL

I don't worry if the flesh
is spirited away some
deep night, if the
following morning splinters
and aerates into mere
fragrance. Metabolism
is just like that. It can't help
being wet any more than
we can help being fleshy.
Or the heron stalking
the air above the lake.
Unless this ends
on an open mouth.

MANHATTANIC

Dried-out jaws of the old pomegranate
on its copper dish should inflect
this desk. How to tell if the
objects here belong? Belong here?
Not simply wondering but
a little *paniqued*. Anything tipped
in metal must be good. Right?
What about intentionality. Compact
sentences assume the fetal
position. A sublet apartment
feels small until you've lived there
for a while, at which point it often
feels smaller.

HOSPITALIST

New definitions of
doing poorly dewing
up on the face.
Not always facing up,
not always aware
of corners, sad
and lite-jazzy.
Aristotle says
thought by itself
moves nothing. No one
decides to have sacked Troy.
All the sounds are in miniature
but the room is large
in ruined light.

THE SELFIST

This narrow fortune, this
hand in absentia. Descent
of any kind, plus ascent.
I feigned a story but it's
all mine, all my mouth.
My spotless love hovers
with white wings. Every piece
of clothing I ever lost
adorns the arm I've got
twisted at my spine.
Darkening stems
of the lower plants—
you'll find me listening
for them to collapse in this heat.

SEX AS IDIOLECT

I can hear the snow rotting
on the pavement, as if in
syllables you can hold in your
mouth. As if the mouth were tuned to
that frequency, a mouth built
for snow, I want all the objects
arranged across your forehead
to lift and then settle back down.
Here is a closed drink, here is the
opposite side of your face, here is
a cab punching through the cold. That
thought got kicked back to the street.

It is imperative that we *sink*,
says Williams in the tall grass.

COLDENED

This says how the red barn is structured by frost

This says how there is always a red barn

This says how this should not prevent us from noticing

This says how there is a clench in morning

This says how coffee stains the water

This says how heat separates the air inside the hotel

This says how salt separates the fish

This says how there is a softness to cold air

This says how Spenser used a fake ancient language

This says how that language strikes us as young

This says how up here in the woods are some thin sticks

This says how the day starts cold and ends cold

This says how there is usually a red barn to the left of the field

THE HOUSE OF ÊTRE

Dear Philadelphia

Dear San Francisco

Dear *Amazing Race*

Dear arbor

Dear ardor

Dear partiality

Dear car on fire

Dear shattered sidewalk

Dear General Douglas MacArthur Tunnel

Dear Borodin Quartet No. 2

Dear *Lost in Space*

Dear Walnut Creek

Dear satellite city

Dear doctor

Dear tanks reading DORMANT OIL

Dear little ghost

Dear Market Street

Dear wine-yellow sea

Dear busted oven

Dear clear medicine

Dear portable coffees

Dear Cégeste

Dear suspended chord

Dear O'Hare

Dear pastel waiting areas

Dear CNN

Dear "foreign" fish

Dear poisoned in Lake Davis

Dear mother tending to cellphone

Dear Aristotle

Dear autobiography

Dear October

Dear clutching

Dear houseless house

Dear shells of leaves

Dear fibery season

Dear suspended fears

Dear animal

Dear icy corners

Dear Emily

Dear seventeen

Dear throwlike

RUINIC

Not automatically thoughtful.
Not precisely tipped in steel.
Lipsticks in stadium-
style seating; the arid
planes of the face; the way
she holds her arms stiffly apart
from her body. All this
hourly aging; the muscles recline in
tired skins. See spine and think
lupine. Is that wishful?
See just the word
and not what stacks atop it.

ETIOLOGICAL

I dipped my hand in the garbage can
and then put my finger in my mouth.
A sort of first self, best self ideological position.

A cold sort of laundry, many masses of cold.
"The shock is how
ordinary it seems."

You think that's all the work you need to do.
You think you can masque it, drinking
from the lake.

That line is exhausting because
most people are not adults.

DIDO

Folded into yellowing mist
she was very good at hiding her feelings.

Anyone could have foretold black wings at dawn;
you don't need tricked-out eyes in your head to see that.

Some of the women say they are sick of struggling
        with the sea.
Who can blame them? A girl can weep sour tears
        for only so long.

Now she says we were never married.
My hands go bone-dry.

Despite the certainty that always accompanies an E-minor descent,
I wasn't expecting things to unfold so literally.

COEVAL

There are nine ways to
fix the edges of the room.
I know you hear it.
Winter pools out
the ear as I walk
west with a hot face.
There's sick in the river.
I've smudged my knees
with a raw perfume. Empty
it out. Glass wipes
clear unless rimmed
out by the glare.

LISTENING TO PAUL ZUKOFSKY PLAY STEFAN WOLPE

The notes sound a bit
sour—I mean they taste
of the air surrounding their
wavering edges. Sometimes
being in an uncluttered place
flips over into tiny jagged dust.
When is it not dragging
the strings. There's a jaunt
to corners that face the bay.
While there's still time, we ought to
get the words all grown up, so we
can hold them in our
own unadorned throats.

HARPSDISCHORD

Here is a book that lights up
every cell of the body. Follow

the directions and you'll be saved.
Edit out each hour. Or each other.

As we gaze at the xrays I feel my
limbs loosen along the saggital plane.

This huckster body, these
visible vessels,
a red chair breathing.

Anybody can write the Californiad.
Just put one color after another.

SERIAL

I'm drawing the same
swath of blue as the night
the room seemed to
pace around me. As if
the air worried. "I hate
the living." First I stepped
gently from the lip of the
plane; then I reorganized
the kitchen attempting
to order time. I threw out
the dead spices, stale water,
frosted meats. I considered
forming an allergy to copper
or else bathing in the street.
Not everything is a citation.

PLANETISH

One's fear is people, going
social. We bruise against
it, or the sun tilts
an array. Nothing false, just
Orpheus's full wrong
divinity, aka manhole. Then
one person says "Your body
is like an anatomy" and
another feels the city reel past
anything calendrical.

Are the letters mammals?
No.
If they could talk, would they be mammals?

SPINAL

And anon as he had said these
words she saw verily how the
air opened bright as any levin.

The chest feels medless but the
spine isn't sure. I leave a small
seam on the fitted sheet where
the dream hunches, clocklike. The
neck turns to check the clock roughly
hourly plus early. It doesn't
turn; its rubbed face
wavers and

anon the creature was stabled
in her wits and in her reason.

LISTENING TO PAUL ZUKOFSKY PLAY PHILIP GLASS

On Locust Street with its low steps
I thought I saw a pastel hotel
settle its elbows onto the walk.
When I talk to you sometimes my tongue
bubbles out of my mouth—I wanted
to say *forth* but it doesn't march, it starts
and stops. The mouth rooted and frothy, lit
with an everyday flavor. The string skips. Paul
Zukofsky's violin stutters. L. says a way
not to feel nervous is to look at the eye.
Hopefully there is a salted sea when you
look there. Horses marching
under their hands. It's never
going to happen.

UNSEASONAL

Bacchus is nothing like the weather.
Flesh is nothing like the weather.

No wait. Deiphobus tells how the
women rained lots of drops.

But that's not technically
the same as weather.

Pretend parties are reasonably rare.
No wait. It's the joy that's rare, not

the trimmings and liquids, not the tables
filled with bits of our matted

intentions. Once someone said love
turned off like a faucet.

I didn't want this
to be that kind of party.

THE NATURAL WORLD

I eat my degrees.
I eat in degrees.

In the dream, her face hangs
on the first quote-unquote
avoidance swept across

a liquid moment, removable
as a piano, trying too hard against

a hell of time or an
unlit ceiling we tried to
keep asleep under
carpeted acousticals
winging back.

THE CORPORATION

A softening or fluidity of the
eye. Lung as punctuation
device. Throat arcing toward
the only way to be in
the poem or outside the
freezer.

What exhausts is terrible
rhythmic presence. That
most people seem adjunct.

Look through that eye, its
closed field. We want
to be delighted. Aftertaste
of antibiotic, vocabularian.

Desires shoal against the flayed
apartment building on
South Street, ATLANTA '96 banner
in a cleaved bedroom. All the
symbolic acts: repair, damage, delay.

What is the corporation.
"I've done a lot of wrong things in my mind."

There's a hot little mouth.
There's a set of swollen pupils

and cash for the passenger.
We're just passengers, we say,
because we don't want to
delight the corporation.

The human hour.
Say it with a certain
Northern Californian
tonalism. Throw out
the hurt piece, let something
flake into the field of vision.

That softening is your
punctuation. Ride it like
it's sustainable.

THE PASSENGER

The first fact is the social body.
Then our arrows point
toward heavy floors,
crash into a sonnet
of little things, etc. A sentence
of long print and its remainders.
At Lake Merced they fire
shots at imaginary birds while
real birds erupt from cypress.
A knot of experience turns inside
the sentence, like how later at the airport
they'll say "There's weather in Pittsburgh."

HAZE

VALLEY FEVER

I was tearing at my cubicle.
Like poor federalism.

All the different *things*
you can't have. Then
to the flood.

A good girl
mixtape.

Dust is like anger, it
can't be rid
of and has
too many
sources

THE FOUR STAGES OF DEPENDENCE

Someone is always mowing in California.
The stumped orange trees propping up winter air.

My eyes feel clean, my forehead scrubbed
with whole ice from the cramped mud.

December twenty-second will be a long
haul even without a freeway.

My newly shorn eyes and a restaurant packed
with red, England on your T-shirt and blood in my

shoe clasping the pads of your fingers in this
apostrophized valley, a well-

hydrated mind and its coordinates
all flat like a piece of laundry.

These new seatbelts are indivisible.
No idea is broken onto two pages.

THE SACRAMENTO OF DESIRE

I left before the makeover ended because the radio
in my rented red Focus would not Seek properly.

Like the song says, me, I play for fortunes.
Sacramento at night is filled with squares of

exhausted air that collect the day's stunted effects.
You with your shoes plucked from overaerated

parking lots of desire; I with my unencumbered hair; vague
figures making a high sound trying to believe their

luck. Bluish variations in cloud movements
seem to function as signs of an end.

I know the structure of what I want to say
but not which fibers, natural or technical.

BAKERSFIELD

Oil pump
in a field of lettuce.

A body repeated
and punched
through paper.

A woolly palm
face up to a road, dry
as winter. Astigmatism
sinking into valley.
Stop trying to
make it happen.

STRATHMORE

Red light followed by white
light, sun turning to snow
in the mouth, new moisture
in the vegetables, dry
docking the encounter, wives,
an idea of the other one, one
window after the other one.

Airports are good places to cry.
Cash for passengers.
The body will always be a
young punctuation device.

DINUBA

Chipped stones, hills, buildings, steps,
gravel, styrofoam, tilted skies,
tilted dust kicking up
and against the valley. Granite's
almost always massive. Orange
trees spiky in the fog. Stray
palms sift off trees,
typing as a way not to talk. I
don't eat theme. These
desks can't support your whole
hurt profile.

TULARE

Stone slab on the midriff, broken
and self-crushed. Fabric on the ice.
A metal wing in flames. This is all happening
right here in the parking lot. Anatomically.
Too much space between the objects;
stories; speech; a concrete floor
which is also a road. And then
the dress also breaking. This is all happening
while fields move toward you
in increments against a weird liquid
thinking about movement.
In flight, ideas get armed: juncture
turns over in the mind before
the place where things meet.
Up in the air now.

VISALIA

An allergy to
bone, this weather.
That's how deep.

Wrong the prepositions.
Are you going to the paper?
Are you opening at the paper?

An unfinished image
floats up to the screen, all
spread across the limpid panel
between car and meridian.

That's too sore and obvious.
As if it moved sleep.
Bring me the arcana.

PORTERVILLE

Granite lining base of the hill,
seam of the car glinting off
seam of the hill and
going very fast. Valley
as prison, valley as door.
Each exit is a lie
yet you have to exit.
Each exit comes hung
low with thick-skinned fruit
worn out by the sun's dull violence.
Oranges limp and roll. As in
a literal face or phantom.
Roadkill lie down.
Trees pile up. Exactly
as do oranges, as down a
granitebed schoolyard, arms
lined up in rows. You have
to exit. Stay in your lines.

McFARLAND

Museum blue lighter than apartment wall but not by much.

That book at the office thicker than your vision but not by much.

The streets faster than your pullups but not by much.

Each email more hysterical than before but not by much.

The room squarer than thought but not by much.

The title more imaginary than dutiful but not by much.

The one mouth more open than the other mouth by a lot.

The street dirtier than the tracks but not by much.

The street like a memory of another street but not really that obvious.

Fabric thick with ice but that's okay.

PROJECTION

One thigh on another thigh and
the last piece of wood
latches shut. A lot of words can
hold, can cross-tune. As we were
in the library, full of
smoke, come down the freeway
at it. Transit and reevaluation. This is the
work right now, to look. Feeling of bread
in the mouth, fog in low steps,
beneath the face a piece of wood, offshoot
of the visible, trajectory of all
these low parts. Tenderness is
a fiction and skin is a boundary.
The library is quite useless.

STRANGE YELLOW FLOWERS

1. Sunshine through the rain

A body wrapped in
leaves, dancers made
of fog, as if the forest
were made from paper.
How to weather weather.
She held one eye
brightly open and
dressed last year like a
wound. We waited
for a tired line
of flowers around
her forehead, a repeated
climax in light's wood.

2. The peach orchard

Quick there's a row of
dusty girls to make you
cry. Pink shadow in
corner and army
waits for Doll Day.
Bring some of the dark
back with you. Waving
my stumped wood
by remote control, dancing
one emergency removed,
I didn't want
to die, here, wetly
and acute. I looked for
a hole in the crowd.

3. The blizzard

There again I've angered
the atmosphere. But still
these hips in a long flurry
of news, a digital you,
then the thing itself.
Sounds as though we're
coughing up snow. As
opposed to all those
blurry lines, I'm just
apartment building.
We froze up to our
kneecaps. Then broke
through that winter bitch.

4. The tunnel

Once you loved all my
last lines. Even the red
here grows dark, we come
bathed in it, or we come
at all. I was wet as
a dog. I'm so sorry, but
you died in my arms.
Sometimes dream dresses
in fact: streetlight swings
through the window, curves
off a table, lands thickly
on regiment. Like how I
tried against the art museum
to eat the menu.

5. Crows

A ripening at the throat
and crying at the dialogic. No
shortage of bones in Van
Gogh's constellation. A body's
injury tells a thousand words
in French. She was a lyrical
socialist. I remind you how
speech catapulted her
through the scar on the canvas.
She had visual tinnitus, or else
night blindness. Then she said
yes. Could you believe it then,
how the sun bleached the sky?

6. Mount Fuji in red

I went on a little retreat.
Things got all melty.
My voice went flat.
They colored radioactivity
on film to catch the sound.
The clouds chased me down.
I got gaunt as fuck
and clipped my forehead.
In the dream I was losing
my hair and saying you don't
understand, I'm losing
my hair.

7. The weeping demon

That park is all white noise.
I think this blue skirt
ordinary in its loveliness.
We feed on ourselves.
Yeah it was a difficult
year but fame catapults
you up and she's always
had an enormous soul.
I pried myself off Tenth
Avenue back when more
persimmons were in
season, lay on top
of the blanket
to save color.

8. Village of the watermills

Birds wave song.
Good water gives
way to a fistful
of bells. Person meets
parade. Why should night
be as bright as day? There's
no getting around this
sweep of frivolity.
As a sidebar, I can offer
one trick by explication.
See, once I pawed at the
door as a liquid building.
Intersubjectivity was optical.

SOUNDS MODERN

Sounds modern
Sounds many
Sounds we can't get our eyes around
Sounds clear
Sounds wet
Sounds eastern edge
Sounds a low chair
Sounds a watery reading
Sounds like it all
Sounds new
Sounds quick
Sounds *lit*
Sounds barbaric
Sounds genius
Sounds toothy
Sounds stolen
Sounds lungy
Sounds raining
Sounds depth
Sounds blank

APOLOGY TO LOS ANGELES

I'm sorry because winter.
I'm sorry because "Lost Angeles."
I'm sorry because the hand is the
most versatile of instruments and even zero
is a position. I'm sorry for the subject
line in the email, the window opened
and a hard piece of metal flew
in from the street, I think
that must have been what happened, just
the dirty structure of everything.
In the mornings the peacocks at Hollywood
Forever walked around and around
in caged circles and I was the cat, I was the house cat.

HOLLYWOOD FOREVER

I don't have a problem with the object.
I don't have a problem with this low
house and its glassy walls. I don't have a problem
with blue jacarandas. I don't have a problem
with performing the longing. I don't
have a problem with the procedure. I
don't have a problem with the No. 4 bus. I
don't have a problem with the current time
as it appears on my arm. I don't have a problem
with "standard American." I don't have a
problem with ideological footwear. I don't
have a problem with anything loose.
I don't have a problem with edges. I don't
have a problem with any gear. I don't
have a problem with an empty house empty
of furniture and words. All the words got
glared out. When you're buried you're
in Hollywood Forever.

ALLISON CORPORATION

ERRINGNESS

I send out signals of a holding kind
but it keeps raining hard outside
the walls of the department building.
Later the machine planes the rain.

How we hunger for modern coffees,
dried household goods. Keats's
lady with her hair in weird syrups is
finally invisible.

Someone plucks out certain
structures of Rachmaninoff's
Prelude No. 3, the one with all the
hammers, while a cup cools on my tray.

It's all apparatus, fine, finally.
The notes are winning, their
errands tuned to the rain.

BLIZZARDISH

Something songy, "having the qualities of song."
More like listening to the martini.
More than the pupils that rise and fall.
More like a set of cheap knives, packed
for the passenger, like the word
"fresh." Say "I think in
cities," but mean "I think about
cities." Streets drenched in white,
whole boroughs wrapping around
our knees, the train drenched
by its tracks.

WOLVERINE

I was only pretending
to be epiphanic

she said, tossing the whole
day over the embankment.

Is the heart collandered
or semiprecious

filled with holes
and therefore filled with light—

this is just the sort of thing
that cannot be said upon a chair

unless that chair is lit up
and wolverine. Can furniture

be wolverine? No, because *wolverine*
is a noun.

FIVE HAWKS

(for Hillary Gravendyk)

I saw five hawks in the sky

HARD LONG

One word leads to the next, then the next
sentence, deep as the stupid sky. I wasn't so much
feeling the anthem, but it was nice of you to
ask. So I'll keep ringing the bell on your arm,
because I'm a made thing, too. Still on the road to
a place-based lie. Because increasing
knowledge leads to atomization?
Because of longing? Seawater?
Everything in Los Angeles is hard and long. All the
fruits are little comets. Going out here is like dressing up
to walk around in your own house.

WHY DO WE STILL LIVE HERE, IN THIS REPULSIVE TOWN?

Everybody's hoarding everything
all the time. Not necessarily headed
toward disaster.

Not necessarily taken from
or stripped of the viral
load of love, a room infected
by the boundaries between objects
now dimming.

The body gets heavy also.
All our friends are in New York.

CHROMOPHILIA

All cells are created equal. Los
Angeles is always moving. Los
Angeles is never moving.

There is a procedure to writing everything down,
setting water on top of a filament and narrowing
the letters to let the time run out.

A cell is a containment.
Fluid rushes in.
It's hard to hinge
on a feeling.
There's pink
in the fabric,
pink
in the lung.

A space between
two people appears too wide.

Everyone's hands move
paperlessly across the field.

We drive unharmed
beneath tinted windows
in this apparently
structureless city.

Change is the subject.
The term is "repetition."

RIGHT OVARY, LEFT OVARY

In dressed-up lips
on a fat planet
in a corner of the belly
a drawn thing beside bone,
not a flat thing, it has to be
quiet here first. This surface
is cluttered. I want to move
to another street. We lost
a crystal in the couch. Some of
the jars were labelled G
and some of the jars were labelled K.

The system sustains itself.
Dan Flavin's fluorescent tubes
are commercially available.

I want to know all the things.
I want to know all the gods.

FOURTH WALK

Don't believe in writing as possession. Don't
believe in bylines like slimming wear.

Store the herbs in a glass jar.
Some are thready, some spiked, some
woody, some grainy, some leafy. This
is a contract. "Green energy" was said on
television in a moment of danger.

Because she wrote it down and it was used as evidence.
Then she spoke and it was recorded.
"Every book is a failure." The way colleges are landscaped
within the context of their pert grasslands.

"We found ourselves repeatedly original."
We felt it necessary to move our legs in rhythm
with all the other limbs in question.
Then we departed the path for the gymnasium,
the steel hips of the elliptical
machine rotating through the air.

"All writing is argument."
They held a hearing test in
one of the last chambers of the university.

You say car. You say house. You say dog. You say
ball. You say apple.

GLASS (FOR THE EYES)

Wood, agave, oil, cloth, glass
for no bland assumption, teeth
down to her waist, clarity
reflects the whole face.

Glass always splinters.
Isn't that shame.

You can choose it, too,
a real girl, on an airplane,
with an aisle seat and everything,
it's your call, just be gentle when you
tear that hunk out the lung

LEFT OVARY, RIGHT OVARY

Because there's so blood.
Hand still cramped, pinned
by wood, opposite the pavement.
Wood on the pavement, blocked out
by a small strung thing—so strung out, like, you know,
all of the lights. It can't hold, or contain,
stuck, previewed on-screen. Or paper,
fine. If you don't understand it's fine.
So, eat lots of ice in wide strips. Just pull up
whole pieces of ice and you'll find a firm object
underneath, a boat or an old chunk of furniture, the kind
we never really look at.

NEGATIVE BRIDE

The desk that swiped my credit card
so sweetly

Fine feeling along this officespace, lazy
capital how are you doing
in this officespace

My body is not a cleaned highway
your body is not a cleaned highway

And yet the officespace cites this body?
How the birds do sing outside the officespace?

Here, take both
pairs of gloves
i.e. hands

WITHOUT CERES AND BACCHUS, VENUS WOULD FREEZE

I know that sonnet because I taught it.
Reddish in that plasticized light.
Not *that* but *how*.
Not so counterfeit as to be smart; just
trying to reel in an offshore frame.
Hard because of all the useless muscles,
not disuse but uselessness, and
stretched thin along pavements battered
by all that recirculates
within the wheel well.
So, because you asked, trying to dip
them back into that ocean
full of smart things and you
have to take
the trash with the salt.
I was the dog we didn't have.

ALLISON CORPORATION

Outside the city is a thick line of thinking
and outside that line of thinking is a strip
of water and outside that strip of water
is a muscle. Lengthen the muscle.
Show restraint and perfect tension. That is
Allison Corporation.

California is not new.
California is not new.
California is not new.

This is a poem for you for you
for spontaneous flight.
Because we live underneath some helicopters.

I'm rewriting the plan.
I'm rewiring the plan.

And outside that muscle is fat and bone
and a car that carries the body elsewhere.

We love the drones.
We love that they all have heads and
arms to fight with. All their
arms are united. You were not
born in California but neither was I.
I am angling at the surface larger

than your actual face, a not
corporate body. This is a love poem
and I did not do any research.

SELECTED NOTES

"Occlusionary": After Elizabeth Hoak Doering's *Dust from 1533, Leonid [Asteroid] Showers*, 2003, drawn by wind, and self-designed apparatus; graphite on mylar.

"Skytime": The word "ingratefull" appears in Aemilia Lanyer's *The Description of Cooke-ham.*

"Dear Mary McDonnell" contains lines from William Wordsworth's *Prelude.*

"The Byronic Woman": "sore sick at heart" and "almost long'd for woe" are from *Childe Harold's Pilgrimage* by George Gordon, Lord Byron.

"PST Sonnet" is a translation of Shakespeare's Sonnet 120 and refers to *Ball Drop*, 1969, by Ron Cooper.

"National Gallery": "You have a very fiery temper according to your hands" was said in conversation by Sueyeun Juliette Lee.

"Hospitalist": Aristotle says "thought by itself moves nothing" and "No one decides to have sacked Troy" in *Nicomachean Ethics.*

"The Selfist": "My spotless love hovers with white wings" is from Samuel Daniel's *Delia.*

"Sex as Idiolect": "It is imperative that we *sink*" is from William Carlos Williams's *In the American Grain.*

"Etiological": "the shock is how ordinary it seems" is from Bob Perelman's "On Don Allen, *The New American Poetry.*"

"Dido" borrows phrases from Edith Hamilton's *Mythology.*

"Serial": "I hate the living" was said by Linda Fiorentino's character in *Men in Black.*

"Planetish": The first two lines are taken from a letter from Lorine Niedecker to Harriet Monroe: "One's fear is people—going social—but now I have another fear: it has been hard to sell magic—will the time come when it can't be *given* away?" "Full wrong divinity" is from Sir Philip Sidney's *The Defense of Poetry.*

"Spinal" contains lines from Margery Kempe's *The Book of Margery Kempe.*

"The Natural World": "hell of time" is from Shakespeare's Sonnet 120.

"The Passenger": "The first fact is the social body" is from Charles Bernstein's "The Kiwi Bird in the Kiwi Tree."

"The Sacramento of Desire": "I play for fortunes" is from Joni Mitchell's "For Free."

"Porterville": "Stay in your lines" is from Eileen Myles's "#11 The Lines."

"Strange Yellow Flowers" is organized by the chapters of and contains lines from Akira Kurosawa's *Dreams.*

"Apology to Los Angeles": "the hand is…" is from Elinor Gadon's *In the Beginning: The Sacred Way of the Goddess*; "Even zero is a position" is from Rachel Blau DuPlessis's *Interstices.*

"Hollywood Forever" contains remarks by Vanessa Place, Dodie Bellamy, Judie Bamber, and Terry Castle at "Q.E.D. Part 3: An Evening of Authentic Objects," hosted by Les Figues Press in Los Angeles, June 2012.

"Erringness": "hair in weird syrups" is from John Keats's *Lamia*.

"Blizzardish": "I think about cities" is from a poem by Carlos Soto Román.

"Why Do We Still Live Here, in this Repulsive Town?": The title and last line are from the song "100,000 Fireflies" by The Magnetic Fields.

"Chromophilia": "apparently structureless" comes from the OED definition of "chromophilic."

"Right Ovary, Left Ovary": Dan Flavin says "The system sustains itself" in reference to his use of fluorescent tubes. Quoted in *Minimalism: Art and Polemics in the Sixties*.

"Fourth Walk": Selected lines and phrases taken from George Orwell, Lisa Robertson, and Jamaica Kincaid.

"Glass (for the eyes)": The title is after the identifying plaque for *Assumption of the Virgin Mary*, anon., 17th c., Qorikancha, Cusco, Peru.

The title of "Negative Bride" is from Jenn McCreary's "thistles, directionless."

ACKNOWLEDGMENTS

Some of the poems in this manuscript, some in previous versions, have appeared in the following publications; I gratefully acknowledge the editors of these publications for publishing them: *Aufgabe*, *Cleaver*, *Comma*, *Poetry*, *Elective Affinities: Cooperative Anthology of Contemporary US Poetry*, *Esque*, *Fact-Simile*, *Involuntary Vision: After Akira Kurosawa's* Dreams (ed. Michael Cross, Avenue B), *The L.A. Telephone Book* (ed. Brian Kim Stefans, Los Angeles), *Manor House Quarterly*, *The Odyssey* (ed. Andrea Lawlor, Pocket Myths), *The Offending Adam*, *Peacock Online Review*, *Peregrine*, *P-Queue*, *Sibila*, *Sidebrow*, *Sixth Finch*, *The Sonnets: Translating and Rewriting Shakespeare* (ed. Paul Legault and Sharmila Cohen, Nightboat/Telephone Books), *Writing from the Inside Out*, and *Zeek*.

Gratitude to all the readers, interlocutors, curators, friends, and editors involved with this book, including: Emily Abendroth, Barbara Joan Tiger Bass, Diana Cage, Maxe Crandall, Sarah Dowling, Hillary Gravendyk, Allison Harris, Dorothea Lasky, Marit MacArthur, Mattilda Bernstein Sycamore, Simone White, and, especially, Rachel Zolf. Deep thanks to Jason, John, and Kris at Sidebrow for their support, editorial acumen, and championing of independent cross-genre work.

Julia Bloch grew up in Northern California and Sydney, Australia, and studied at Carleton College, Mills College, and the University of Pennsylvania. She is the author most recently of the book *Letters to Kelly Clarkson* (Sidebrow Books), a finalist for the Lambda Literary Award, and the Little Red Leaves chapbook *Hollywood Forever*. Her poetry, reviews, and essays have appeared in *Aufgabe, The Volta, Journal of Modern Literature*, and elsewhere; she is the recipient of the San Francisco Foundation's Joseph Henry Jackson Literary Award and the William Carlos Williams Prize for Poetry. For two years she taught literature at the Bard College MAT program in Delano, California, and now lives in Philadelphia, where she teaches literature and creative writing at the University of Pennsylvania and is an editor at *Jacket2*.

SIDEBROW BOOKS | www.sidebrow.net

SIDEBROW 01 ANTHOLOGY
*A multi-threaded, collaborative
narrative featuring work by 65 writers*
SB001 | ISBN: 0-9814975-0-0

SPED
Teresa K. Miller
SB008 | ISBN: 0-9814975-7-8

**ON WONDERLAND
& WASTE**
Sandy Florian
Collages by Alexis Anne Mackenzie
SB002 | ISBN: 0-9814975-1-9

**BEYOND THIS POINT
ARE MONSTERS**
Roxanne Carter
SB009 | ISBN: 0-9814975-8-6

SELENOGRAPHY
Joshua Marie Wilkinson
Polaroids by Tim Rutili
SB003 | ISBN: 0-9814975-2-7

**THE COURIER'S
ARCHIVE & HYMNAL**
Joshua Marie Wilkinson
SB010 | ISBN: 0-9814975-9-4

NONE OF THIS IS REAL
Miranda Mellis
SB005 | ISBN: 0-9814975-4-3

**FOR ANOTHER
WRITING BACK**
Elaine Bleakney
SB011 | ISBN: 1-940090-00-8

**LETTERS TO
KELLY CLARKSON**
Julia Bloch
SB007 | ISBN: 0-9814975-6-X

THE VOLTA BOOK OF POETS
*A constellation of the most innovative
poetry evolving today, featuring 50 poets of
disparate backgrounds and traditions*
SB012 | ISBN: 1-940090-01-6

To order, and to view our entire catalog, including new
and forthcoming titles, visit www.sidebrow.net/books.